CHILDREN's DINOSAUR ATLAS

CONTENTS

Written by John Malam • Illustrated by Katrin Wiehle & Simon Morse

HOW TO USE THE ATLAS

An atlas is a book of maps. This atlas is divided into 10 different regions that make up our planet. Each map is marked with country borders, oceans, major rivers, lakes, and mountains. This is the world we know, but it is nothing like the world of the dinosaurs. These prehistoric reptiles ruled the world for about 175 million years, until they died out about 65 million years ago. In all that time, the continents changed their shape and positions on the Earth's surface (see page 6). Each dinosaur image on the map shows you where its fossil was found.

Key to the maps

- Rivers
- Mountains
- Country borders
- Lakes

Important dinosaur locations
Some of the world's most famous dinosaur locations are shown on this map of the world.

North America
1. Dinosaur Provincial Park, Alberta, Canada
2. Petrified Forest, Arizona
3. Ghost Ranch, New Mexico
4. Dinosaur Monument, Colorado
5. Cedar Mountain, Utah
6. Hell Creek, Montana

South America
7. Valley of the Moon, Argentina
8. Auca Mahuevo, Argentina
9. Araripe Basin, Brazil

Europe
10. Solnhofen, Germany
11. Hateg Island, Romania

Africa
12. Tendaguru, Tanzania
13. Bahariya Oasis, Egypt

Asia
14. Lufeng Basin, China
15. Dashanpu, China
16. Liaoning, China
17. Gobi Desert, Mongolia

Australia and Antarctica
18. Dinosaur Cove, Australia
19. Fossil Triangle, Australia
20. James Ross Island, Antarctica

Dinosaurs lived here

Dinosaur fossils are found on all seven of Earth's continents, including Antarctica, the frozen continent. But they are only found in places where the rocks are of the correct age, dating from about 250 million to 65 million years ago. If the rocks are older or younger than this, there will be no dinosaur fossils there. It's for this reason that dinosaur fossils are found in some places, and not in others.

Dinosaur Spotter's Guide

Find out more about some of the dinosaurs that lived on each continent. Complete the quiz and add the correct sticker in the space above each question.

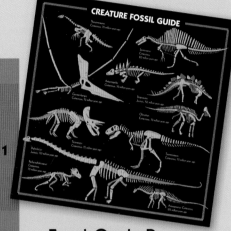

Fossil Guide Poster

Learn about the different types of dinosaurs and their fossils, with this illustrated fold-out poster.

The compass

Each map has a compass to show which way is north, south, east, and west.

Dinosaur Stickers

Complete the maps by adding the stickers: find the right ones and stick them into the spaces marked by dotted lines. There are also stickers for free play.

Where in the world?

Each map includes a mini world map that shows the featured region in color.

Map coordinates

Use the numbers and letters around the edge of the map to describe where to find a dinosaur. For example, the compass symbol is at 2H.

A CHANGING WORLD

Earth is a restless planet. Over millions of years powerful forces of nature have been at work. They've slowly shaped the land and sea, forming the continents and oceans we know today. Travel back in time to when dinosaurs roamed the Earth, and the world was a very different place.

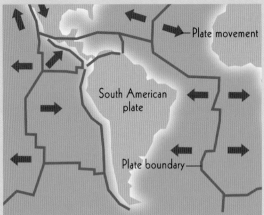

Plate movement

South American plate

Plate boundary

Continents on the move

The surface, or crust, of the Earth is divided into large pieces of land called plates. The continents lie on top of the plates, and because the plates are slowly moving, the continents move with them.

**Triassic Period
250-200 million
years ago**

Single continent

All land on Earth was once joined together into a massive super-continent surrounded by ocean, known as Pangaea, meaning "All Earth." The very first dinosaurs appeared on Pangaea during the Triassic Period, about 230 million years ago.

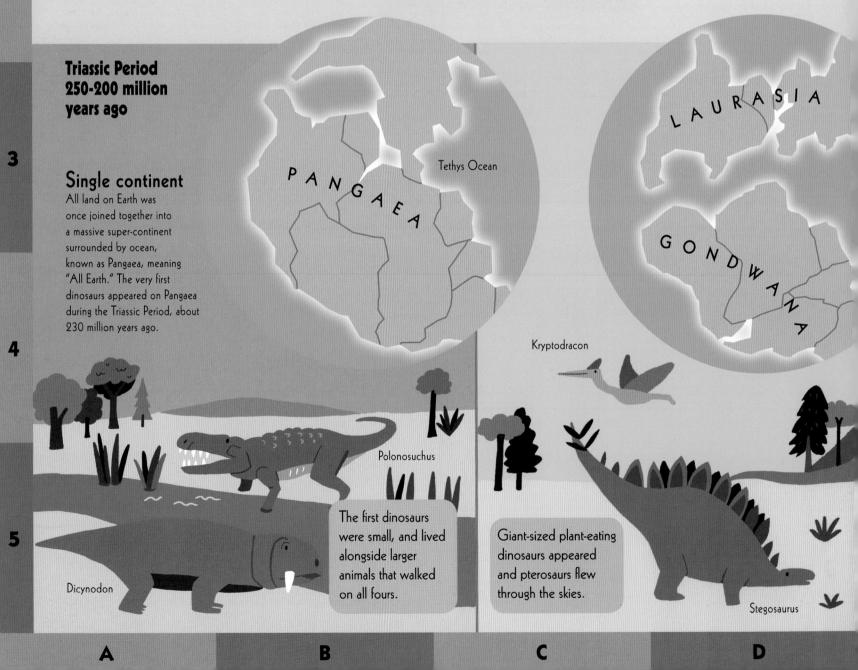

PANGAEA

Tethys Ocean

LAURASIA

GONDWANA

Kryptodracon

Polonosuchus

Dicynodon

The first dinosaurs were small, and lived alongside larger animals that walked on all fours.

Giant-sized plant-eating dinosaurs appeared and pterosaurs flew through the skies.

Stegosaurus

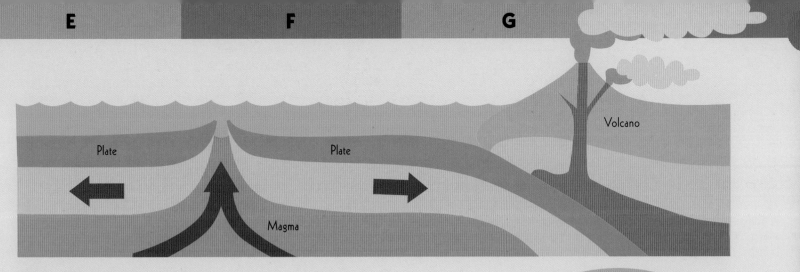

Volcano

Plate → Plate

← Magma

Why the continents move

In the oceans, magma, which is molten rock from deep inside the planet, is constantly forced up to the surface by plates sliding over each other. As the magma hardens to make new crust, it pushes the older crust down. It's this constant cycle of making new crust that causes the Earth's plates—and the continents—to move.

North America

Europe

Asia

South America

Africa

India

Antarctica

Australia

Jurassic Period
200-145 million years ago

Two continents

The Pangaea super-continent started to break into two separate land masses, which slowly moved away from each other. In the northern part of the world was the giant continent known as Laurasia, and in the south was Gondwana. Reptiles ruled the Earth— dinosaurs lived on the land, pterosaurs were masters of the sky, and plesiosaurs inhabited the ocean.

Cretaceous Period
145-65 million years ago

Continents form

As Laurasia and Gondwana moved apart, they broke up into smaller pieces, which eventually became the continents we have today (Asia, Africa, North America, South America, Antarctica, Europe, and Australia). Dinosaurs lived on every continent and were the most successful animals on land.

Fierce meat-eating dinosaurs hunted and scavenged for prey. Some dinosaurs developed body armor for protection.

Tethys Ocean

Microraptor

Diplodocus

Tyrannosaurus rex

Tree ferns

Parasaurolophus

Allosaurus

Magnolia

WHAT IS A DINOSAUR?

Dinosaurs died out about 65 million years ago, and everything we know about them has come from studying their fossils—bones, teeth, eggs, footprints, and whatever else has been preserved. So far, scientists have discovered about 2,000 different kinds of dinosaur, and more new species are found every year.

Scientists use the following basic rules to define what dinosaurs are:

- Dinosaurs lived between 240 and 65 million years ago.
- Dinosaurs had straight legs tucked underneath their bodies.
- Dinosaurs only lived on land.
- Dinosaurs were reptiles.

Stegosaurus
"roofed lizard"

Acrocanthosaurus
"top lizard"

Diplodocus
"double beam"

Theropod

"Terrible lizards"

In 1842, English scientist Richard Owen invented a new word—"dinosaur." He had been studying the fossilized bones of mysterious animals, and the more he looked at the old bones, the more certain he was that they came from a new animal group. The group needed a name, so Owen put two Greek words together—deinos, meaning "terrible," and sauros, meaning "lizard."

Reptiles and other animals

Many other animals lived at the same time as dinosaurs, but reptiles were the dominant animals on land, in the sea, and in the sky. Sea-dwelling reptiles, such as dolphinlike icthyosaurs, long-necked plesiosaurs, and fierce pliosaurs, ruled the seas. The sky was home to pterosaurs—flying reptiles with leathery wings, teeth, and claws. These reptiles shared their world with small mammals, such as the shrewlike Megazostrodon, and countless numbers of dragonflies and other insects.

Ichthyosaurus

Dragonfly

Pterosaur

Megazostrodon

Sauropod

Theropods and sauropods

Dinosaurs belong to one of two groups, depending on the shape of their hip bones. One group had hip bones shaped like those of lizards, the other group had hip bones like those of birds. The lizard-hipped dinosaurs can be divided into meat-eaters (theropods) and plant-eaters (sauropods).

Dinosaur Bones

Fossilized bones are the most important source of information about dinosaurs. By piecing them together, scientists build up dinosaur skeletons, which can then be studied.

A   B   C   D   E

1

2

3

4

NORTH AMERICA

North America has a rich dinosaur fossil record, with a great diversity of dinosaurs stretching from the north of Canada all the way down to Central America. This includes two of the world's greatest fossil sites in Alberta, Canada and Hell Creek, USA. Mexico figures prominently in the history of dinosaurs because it is where a giant asteroid hit the Earth 65 million years ago. It is believed this triggered the mass extinction of dinosaurs.

FACT FILE

Largest meat eater
Tyrannosaurus rex: up to 18,000 pounds
Longest plant eater
Diplodocus: about 125 feet
Fastest land dinosaur
Ornithomimus: up to 25 mph
Smallest brains compared to size
Stegosaurus: 2.6 ounces to 6,800 pounds

Dinosaur Park

Dinosaur Provincial Park in Alberta, Canada, is the site of the greatest number of dinosaur finds in the world. Over 50 dinosaur fossils have been discovered here, including the fierce Gorgosaurus, the small, thick-skulled Pachycephalosaurus, and the spiked Styracosaurus (all pictured, right).

Pteranodon

Ankylosaurus

Ankylosaurus

Hadrosaur

Styracosaurus

Albertonykus

Gorgosaurus

Pachycephalosaurus

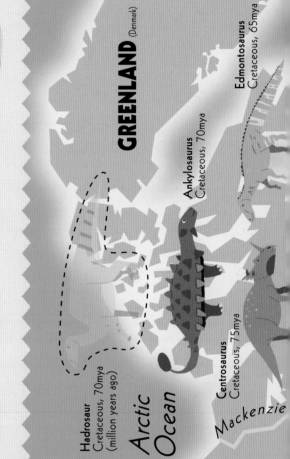

GREENLAND (Denmark)

Hadrosaur
Cretaceous, 70mya
(million years ago)

Ankylosaurus
Cretaceous, 70mya

Edmontosaurus
Cretaceous, 65mya

Arctic Ocean

Centrosaurus
Cretaceous, 75mya

Mackenzie

Alaska (USA)

Pachycephalosaurus
Cretaceous, 70mya

Yuko

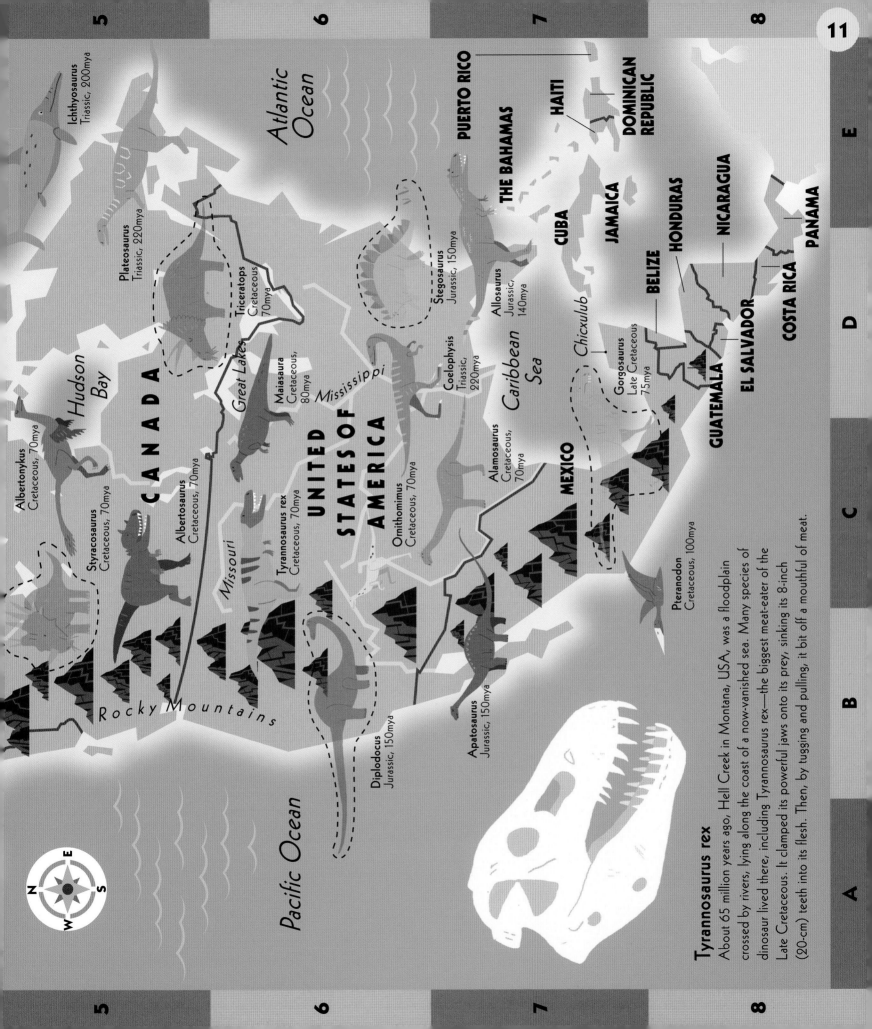

Ichthyosaurus
Triassic, 200mya

Atlantic Ocean

PUERTO RICO

THE BAHAMAS

HAITI

DOMINICAN REPUBLIC

CUBA

JAMAICA

HONDURAS

NICARAGUA

BELIZE

Platesaurus
Triassic, 220mya

Triceratops
Cretaceous,
70mya

Stegosaurus
Jurassic, 150mya

Allosaurus
Jurassic,
140mya

Hudson Bay

Great Lakes

Chicxulub

EL SALVADOR

COSTA RICA

PANAMA

Albertonykus
Cretaceous, 70mya

Styracosaurus
Cretaceous, 70mya

C A N A D A

Maiasaura
Cretaceous,
80mya

Mississippi

Coelophysis
Triassic,
220mya

Caribbean Sea

Gorgosaurus
Late Cretaceous
75mya

GUATEMALA

Albertosaurus
Cretaceous, 70mya

Tyrannosaurus rex
Cretaceous, 70mya

U N I T E D

S T A T E S   O F

A M E R I C A

Ornithomimus
Cretaceous, 70mya

Alamosaurus
Cretaceous,
70mya

MEXICO

Missouri

Pteranodon
Cretaceous, 100mya

Rocky Mountains

Diplodocus
Jurassic, 150mya

Apatosaurus
Jurassic, 150mya

Pacific Ocean

Tyrannosaurus rex

About 65 million years ago, Hell Creek in Montana, USA, was a floodplain crossed by rivers, lying along the coast of a now-vanished sea. Many species of dinosaur lived there, including Tyrannosaurus rex—the biggest meat-eater of the Late Cretaceous. It clamped its powerful jaws onto its prey, sinking its 8-inch (20-cm) teeth into its flesh. Then, by tugging and pulling, it bit off a mouthful of meat.

N
E
W
S

SOUTH AMERICA

Some of the dinosaurs of South America are similar to those found in Africa. This is because at one time the two continents were joined together, and dinosaurs could travel across one great landmass. Many of South America's dinosaurs were found in Argentina, and one of them, Eoraptor ("Dawn thief"), lived about 225 million years ago. The tiny dinosaur was one of the world's very first meat-eating dinosaurs.

FACT FILE

Oldest
Herrerasaurus and Eoraptor: lived 225 million years ago

Biggest meat-eater
Giganotosaurus: 43 feet long with 8-inch sharp teeth

Did you know?
Scientists were so irritated that someone had faked the snout of a new dinosaur from Brazil with car body filler, they named it Irritator!

Caribbean Sea

North Atlantic Ocean

Pacific Ocean

VENEZUELA

COLOMBIA

ECUADOR

PERU

GUYANA

SURINAME

FRENCH GUIANA

BRAZIL

Orinoco

Magdalena

Japurá

Maranon

Amazon

Juruá

Purus

Amazon

Rio Negro

Rio Grande

Lake Titicaca

Guaporé

Madeira

Tocantins

Xingu

São Francisco

Santanaraptor
Cretaceous, 110mya

Mirischia
Cretaceous, 105mya

Irritator
Cretaceous, 100mya

Amazonsaurus
Cretaceous, 100mya

N E S W

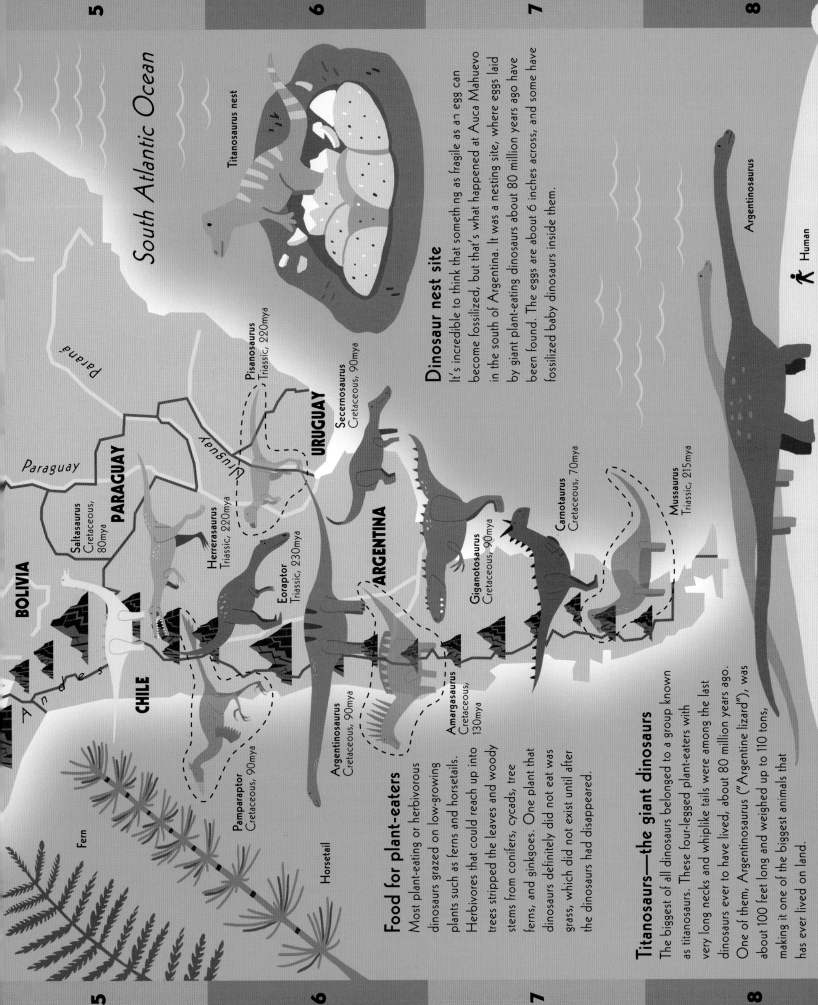

South Atlantic Ocean

Titanosaurus nest

Paraná

Paraguay

Uruguay

PARAGUAY

BOLIVIA

URUGUAY

CHILE

ARGENTINA

Andes

Fern

Horsetail

Saltasaurus
Cretaceous,
80mya

Herrerasaurus
Triassic, 220mya

Eoraptor
Triassic, 230mya

Pisanosaurus
Triassic, 220mya

Secernosaurus
Cretaceous, 90mya

Pamparaptor
Cretaceous, 90mya

Argentinosaurus
Cretaceous, 90mya

Amargasaurus
Cretaceous,
130mya

Giganotosaurus
Cretaceous, 90mya

Carnotaurus
Cretaceous, 70mya

Mussaurus
Triassic, 215mya

Argentinosaurus

Human

A   B   C   D   E

Dinosaur nest site

It's incredible to think that something as fragile as an egg can become fossilized, but that's what happened at Auca Mahuevo in the south of Argentina. It was a nesting site, where eggs laid by giant plant-eating dinosaurs about 80 million years ago have been found. The eggs are about 6 inches across, and some have fossilized baby dinosaurs inside them.

Food for plant-eaters

Most plant-eating or herbivorous dinosaurs grazed on low-growing plants such as ferns and horsetails. Herbivores that could reach up into trees stripped the leaves and woody stems from conifers, cycads, tree ferns, and ginkgoes. One plant that dinosaurs definitely did not eat was grass, which did not exist until after the dinosaurs had disappeared.

Titanosaurs—the giant dinosaurs

The biggest of all dinosaurs belonged to a group known as titanosaurs. These four-legged plant-eaters with very long necks and whiplike tails were among the last dinosaurs ever to have lived, about 80 million years ago. One of them, Argentinosaurus ("Argentine lizard"), was about 100 feet long and weighed up to 110 tons, making it one of the biggest animals that has ever lived on land.

NORTHERN EUROPE

Europe's first dinosaurs appeared about 225 million years ago, toward the end of the Triassic Period. At this time, Europe was at the northern edge of the Pangaea super-continent, lying close to the Equator, where the climate was hot and dry. Dinosaur fossils have been found at many sites in northern Europe, particularly in Germany, France, and southern England—but there are many parts of the continent where none are found at all.

Scaphognathus

Juravenator

Archaeopteryx

FACT FILE

First named
Megalosaurus: named in 1824
Biggest footprints
An unknown giant dinosaur left 6.5-foot wide footprints in eastern France.
Did you know?
Archaeopteryx was a primitive, birdlike dinosaur that used claws on its toes and fingers to climb up trees, from where it made a short, flapping glide.

Gyrodus

Eryonid Crab

vian Mountains

Lepidotes

Aspidorhynchus

Starfish

Solnhofen, southern Germany

The fossils of more than 500 different animal species have been found in limestone rocks at Solnhofen, southern Germany. About 150 million years ago the area was a lagoon of salty water, where fish, turtles, starfish, jellyfish, ammonites, and worms lived. In the sky above flew pterosaurs and a primitive bird called Archaeopteryx. Their dead bodies sank to the bottom of the lagoon, where they were slowly fossilized. The Solnhofen site has produced some of Europe's best-preserved fossils.

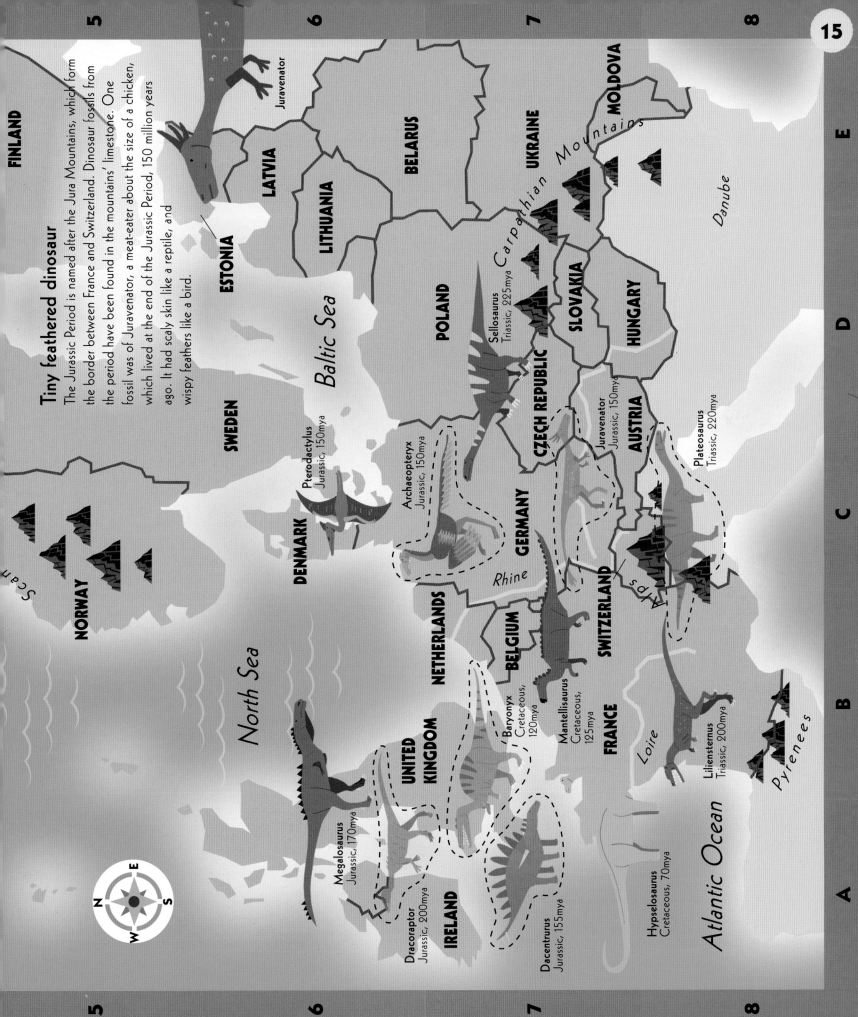

15

Tiny feathered dinosaur

The Jurassic Period is named after the Jura Mountains, which form the border between France and Switzerland. Dinosaur fossils from the period have been found in the mountains' limestone. One fossil was of Juravenator, a meat-eater about the size of a chicken, which lived at the end of the Jurassic Period, 150 million years ago. It had scaly skin like a reptile, and wispy feathers like a bird.

FINLAND

NORWAY

SWEDEN

ESTONIA

LATVIA

LITHUANIA

BELARUS

DENMARK

Pterodactylus
Jurassic, 150mya

Baltic Sea

POLAND

UKRAINE

MOLDOVA

Carpathian Mountains

Danube

Sellosaurus
Triassic, 225mya

SLOVAKIA

HUNGARY

AUSTRIA

Plateosaurus
Triassic, 220mya

Juravenator
Jurassic, 150mya

CZECH REPUBLIC

GERMANY

Archaeopteryx
Jurassic, 150mya

Rhine

Alps

SWITZERLAND

NETHERLANDS

BELGIUM

Baryonyx
Cretaceous,
120mya

Mantellisaurus
Cretaceous,
125mya

FRANCE

Loire

North Sea

Megalosaurus
Jurassic, 170mya

UNITED KINGDOM

Dracoraptor
Jurassic, 200mya

IRELAND

Dacentrurus
Jurassic, 155mya

Hypselosaurus
Cretaceous, 70mya

Liliensternus
Triassic, 200mya

Pyrenees

Atlantic Ocean

Scan

Juravenator

N E S W

5 6 7 8

A B C D E

A   B   C   D

SOUTHERN EUROPE

Spain, Portugal, and Romania are the main locations for dinosaur fossils in southern and central Europe. Tens of thousands of melon-sized dinosaur eggs have been found at a site in the north of Spain, laid in nests by giant plant-eating sauropods about 70 million years ago. Dinosaur footprints and tracks have been found in Portugal, and in Romania there's an island site famous for dwarf dinosaurs.

FACT FILE

Biggest plant-eater
Turiasaurus: 130 feet long, 50 tons

Biggest meat-eater
Torvosaurus: 4-inch bladelike teeth

Did you know?
Hypsilophodon, from Spain, was a plant-eating two-legged dinosaur that lived in herds and was built for speed —it may have run at up to 23 mph.

Atlantic Ocean

N W E S

Allosaurus
Cretaceous, 140mya

Blaisaurus
Cretaceous, 65mya

Pyrenees

Torvosaurus
Jurassic, 150mya

Stegosaurus
Cretaceous, 140mya

Turiasaurus
Jurassic, 145mya

PORTUGAL

Draconyx
Jurassic, 150mya

SPAIN

Ceratosaurus
Jurassic, 150mya

Pelecanimimus
Cretaceous, 130mya

Hypsilophodon
Cretaceous, 120mya

Wings Across Europe

Pterosaurs flew across land and sea, and their fossils have been found in several places in Europe. One of the largest of all pterosaurs was Hatzegopteryx, whose wings measured 46 feet tip to tip and whose skull was 8 feet long. Fossils of this giant flyer have been found in Romania. It probably lived off fish and small land animals.

Hatzegopteryx

A   B   C   D

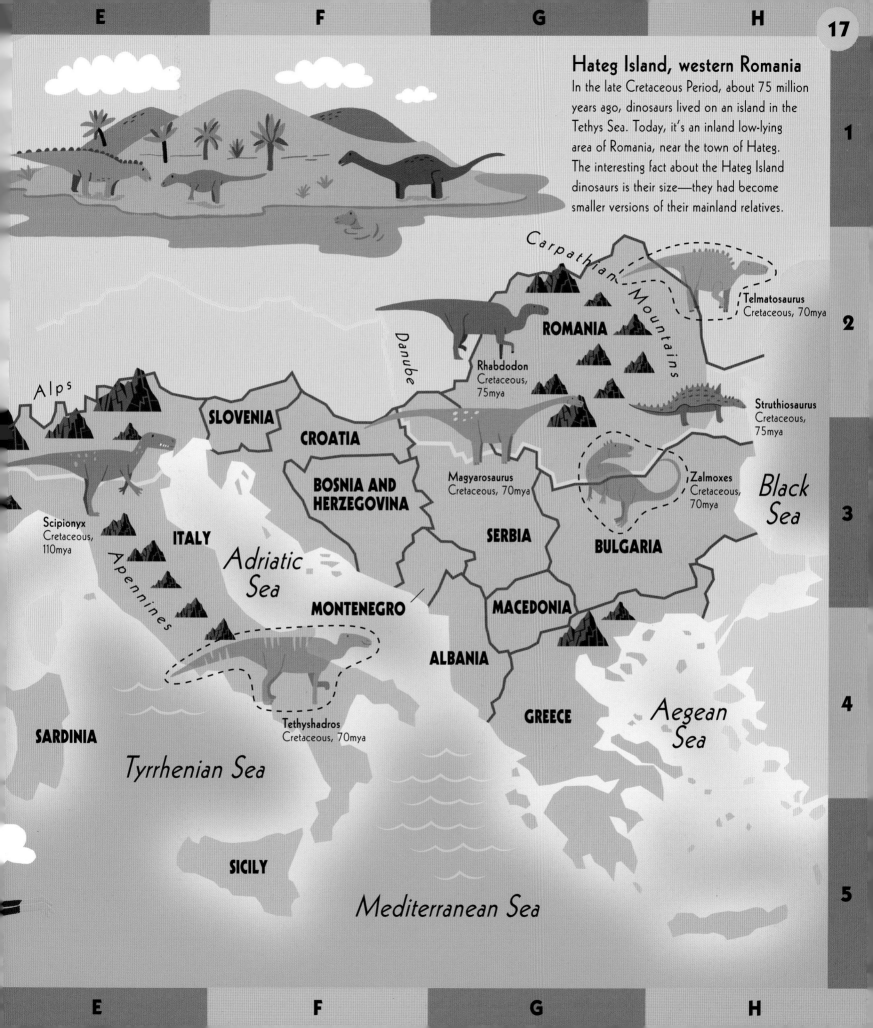

Hateg Island, western Romania

In the late Cretaceous Period, about 75 million years ago, dinosaurs lived on an island in the Tethys Sea. Today, it's an inland low-lying area of Romania, near the town of Hateg. The interesting fact about the Hateg Island dinosaurs is their size—they had become smaller versions of their mainland relatives.

Carpathian Mountains

Telmatosaurus
Cretaceous, 70mya

ROMANIA

Danube

Rhabdodon
Cretaceous,
75mya

Struthiosaurus
Cretaceous,
75mya

Alps

SLOVENIA

CROATIA

Magyarosaurus
Cretaceous, 70mya

Zalmoxes
Cretaceous,
70mya

Black
Sea

BOSNIA AND
HERZEGOVINA

Scipionyx
Cretaceous,
110mya

ITALY

Adriatic
Sea

SERBIA

BULGARIA

Apennines

MONTENEGRO

MACEDONIA

Tethyshadros
Cretaceous, 70mya

ALBANIA

GREECE

Aegean
Sea

SARDINIA

Tyrrhenian Sea

SICILY

Mediterranean Sea

AFRICA

One of the world's first dinosaurs lived in Africa—a small plant-eater called Nyasasaurus. Found in the present-day country of Tanzania, Nyasasaurus roamed across the land 240 million years ago. Tanzania, in East Africa, has produced some of the continent's most famous dinosaurs of the Jurassic Period, from a site at Tendaguru Hill where a 150-million-year-old dinosaur graveyard has been discovered.

FACT FILE

Longest spines
Kentrosaurus: bony tail spines up to 24 inches long

Heaviest plant-eater
Paralititan: weighed up to 88 tons

Did you know?
Brachiosaurus, from Tanzania, was a giant plant-eating dinosaur that needed to eat about 440 pounds of plants every day!

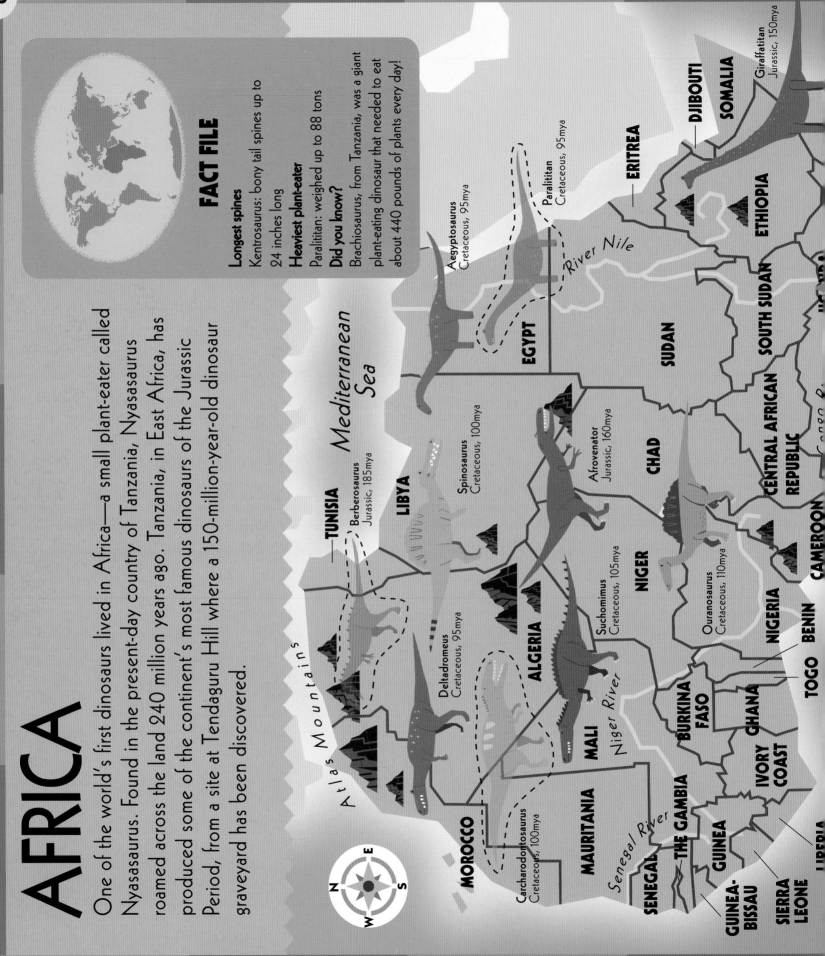

Mediterranean Sea

Atlas Mountains

River Nile

Niger River

Senegal River

MOROCCO

TUNISIA
Berberosaurus
Jurassic, 185mya

LIBYA

Spinosaurus
Cretaceous, 100mya

EGYPT

Aegyptosaurus
Cretaceous, 95mya

Paralititan
Cretaceous, 95mya

ERITREA

DJIBOUTI

SOMALIA

ETHIOPIA

Giraffatitan
Jurassic, 150mya

SOUTH SUDAN

SUDAN

CHAD

Afrovenator
Jurassic, 160mya

CENTRAL AFRICAN
REPUBLIC

Deltadromeus
Cretaceous, 95mya

ALGERIA

MALI

NIGER

Suchomimus
Cretaceous, 105mya

NIGERIA

Ouranosaurus
Cretaceous, 110mya

CAMEROON

BENIN

TOGO

GHANA

IVORY
COAST

BURKINA
FASO

GUINEA

THE GAMBIA

MAURITANIA

Carcharodontosaurus
Cretaceous, 100mya

SENEGAL

GUINEA-
BISSAU

SIERRA
LEONE

LIBERIA

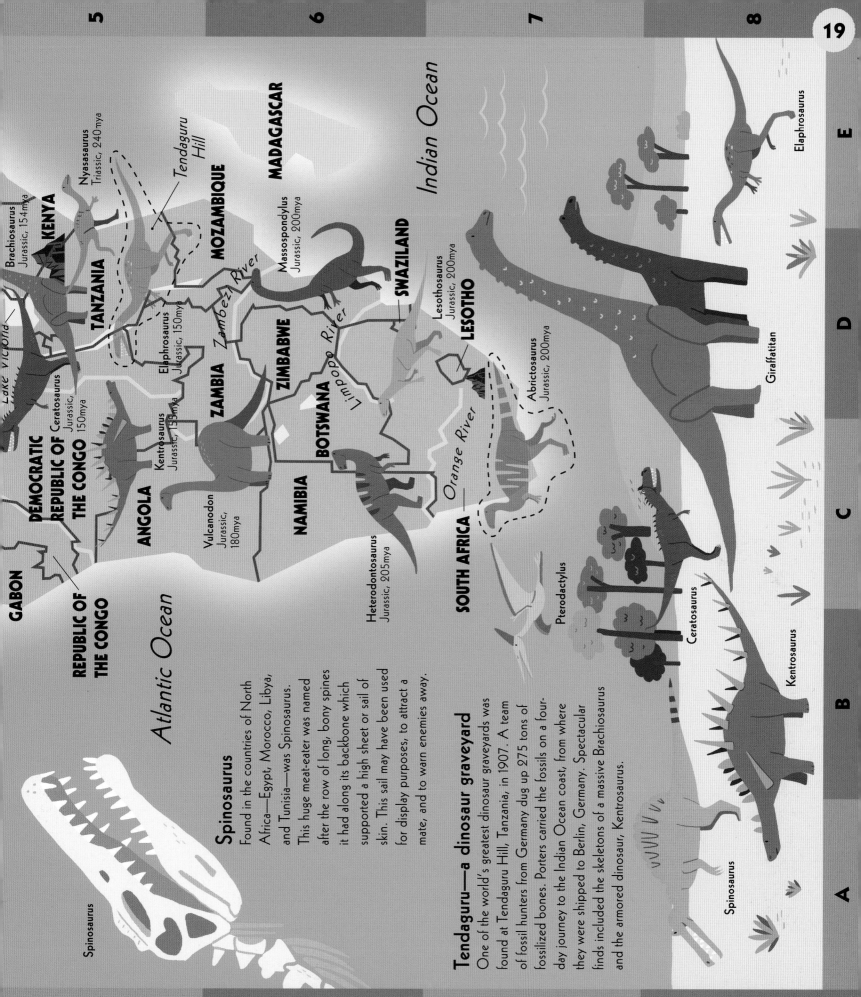

KENYA

Brachiosaurus
Jurassic, 154mya

Nyasasaurus
Triassic, 240mya

Tendaguru
Hill

MOZAMBIQUE

MADAGASCAR

Massospondylus
Jurassic, 200mya

TANZANIA

Zambezi River

Elaphrosaurus
Jurassic, 150mya

SWAZILAND

Indian Ocean

Ceratosaurus,
Jurassic,
150mya

ZAMBIA

Kentrosaurus
Jurassic, 155mya

Limpopo River

Lesothosaurus
Jurassic, 200mya

LESOTHO

**DEMOCRATIC
REPUBLIC OF
THE CONGO**

Lake Victoria

ZIMBABWE

Abrictosaurus
Jurassic, 200mya

GABON

ANGOLA

Vulcanodon
Jurassic,
180mya

BOTSWANA

Orange River

**REPUBLIC OF
THE CONGO**

Atlantic Ocean

NAMIBIA

SOUTH AFRICA

Pterodactylus

Heterodontosaurus
Jurassic, 205mya

Giraffatitan

Spinosaurus

Found in the countries of North
Africa—Egypt, Morocco, Libya,
and Tunisia—was Spinosaurus.
This huge meat-eater was named
after the row of long, bony spines
it had along its backbone which
supported a high sheet or sail of
skin. This sail may have been used
for display purposes, to attract a
mate, and to warn enemies away.

Tendaguru—a dinosaur graveyard

One of the world's greatest dinosaur graveyards was
found at Tendaguru Hill, Tanzania, in 1907. A team
of fossil hunters from Germany dug up 275 tons of
fossilized bones. Porters carried the fossils on a four-
day journey to the Indian Ocean coast, from where
they were shipped to Berlin, Germany. Spectacular
finds included the skeletons of a massive Brachiosaurus
and the armored dinosaur, Kentrosaurus.

Spinosaurus

Ceratosaurus

Kentrosaurus

Spinosaurus

Elaphrosaurus

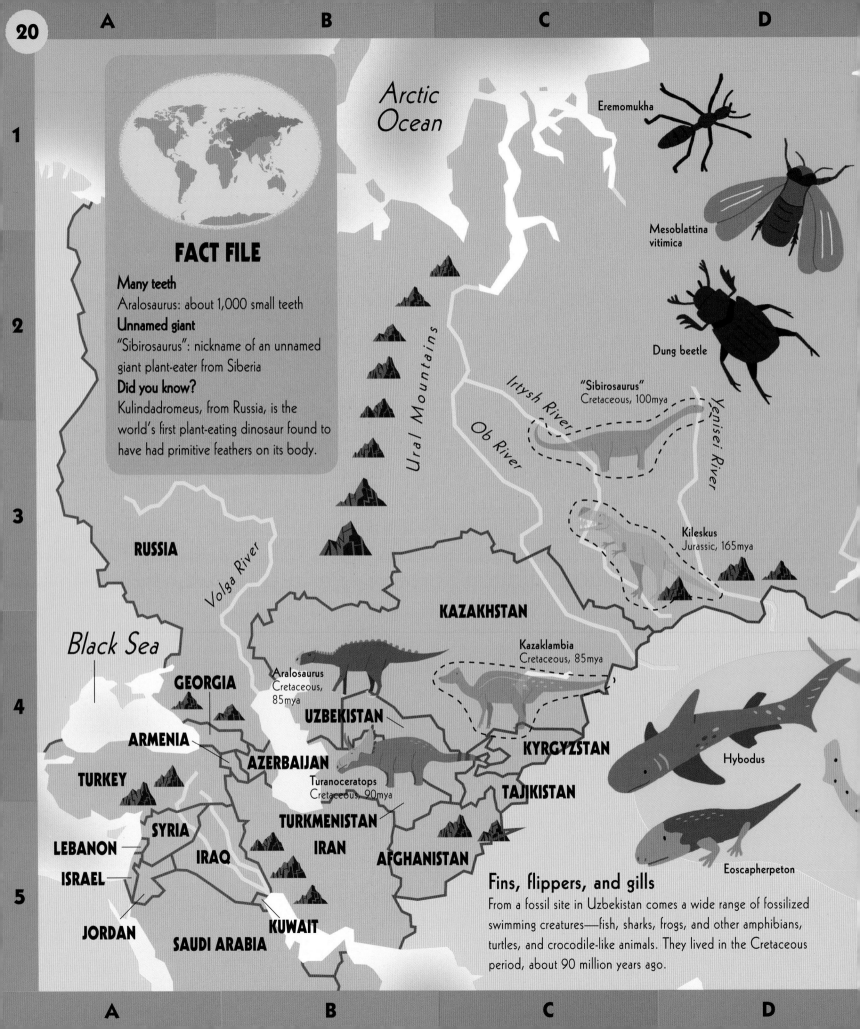

A B C D

Arctic Ocean

Eremomukha

Mesoblattina vitimica

Dung beetle

FACT FILE

Many teeth
Aralosaurus: about 1,000 small teeth

Unnamed giant
"Sibirosaurus": nickname of an unnamed giant plant-eater from Siberia

Did you know?
Kulindadromeus, from Russia, is the world's first plant-eating dinosaur found to have had primitive feathers on its body.

Ural Mountains

Irtysh River

Ob River

Yenisei River

"Sibirosaurus"
Cretaceous, 100mya

Kileskus
Jurassic, 165mya

RUSSIA

Volga River

KAZAKHSTAN

Kazaklambia
Cretaceous, 85mya

Black Sea

GEORGIA

Aralosaurus
Cretaceous,
85mya

UZBEKISTAN

ARMENIA

AZERBAIJAN

KYRGYZSTAN

TURKEY

Turanoceratops
Cretaceous, 90mya

Hybodus

TAJIKISTAN

SYRIA

TURKMENISTAN

LEBANON

IRAQ

IRAN

AFGHANISTAN

ISRAEL

Fins, flippers, and gills
From a fossil site in Uzbekistan comes a wide range of fossilized swimming creatures—fish, sharks, frogs, and other amphibians, turtles, and crocodile-like animals. They lived in the Cretaceous period, about 90 million years ago.

JORDAN

KUWAIT

Eoscapherpeton

SAUDI ARABIA

A B C D

Arctic Ocean

Strashila
incredibili

Beetles, flies, and bugs

In the north of Russia is the vast
region of Siberia, and it's here that
some of the world's best-preserved
insect fossils are found. At a site
along the Vitim River, thousands of
flying and crawling insects that lived
alongside the dinosaurs have been
uncovered, in rocks that are about
80 million years old.

Saurodectes
vrsanskyi

Chersky Range

Kolyma Range

Lena River

Pacific Ocean

Vitim River

Kerberosaurus
Cretaceous, 65mya

Amurosaurus
Cretaceous, 70mya

Olorotitan
Cretaceous, 70mya

Nipponosaurus
Cretaceous, 65mya

Kulindadromeus
Jurassic, 160mya

Kundurosaurus
Cretaceous, 65mya

RUSSIA AND
EURASIA

Kansajsuchus

Compared with other parts of the world, relatively few
dinosaur fossils have been found in Russia and neighboring
countries. Most fossils of land animals found in Russia come
from the time before the dinosaurs. However, new finds of
feathered, plant-eating dinosaurs from Siberia show that there
could be much more to be found here.

Heterodontus
francisci

East China Sea

A B C D E
1 2 3 4

INDIA AND MADAGASCAR

The story of India's dinosaurs begins in the Late Triassic period, about 220 million years ago, when Alwalkeria—an omnivore that ate both meat and plants—ran across the land. At that time, Madagascar was connected to India on the super-continent, Pangaea, before it broke apart. Today, Madagascar is an island off the east coast of Africa, but its dinosaurs are like those found in India.

FACT FILE

Oldest
Alwalkeria: lived 230 million years ago

Most complete skeleton
Barapasaurus: only its skull and a tail bone are missing

Did you know?
Hundreds of dinosaur eggs as big as footballs have been found at a site in the west of India.

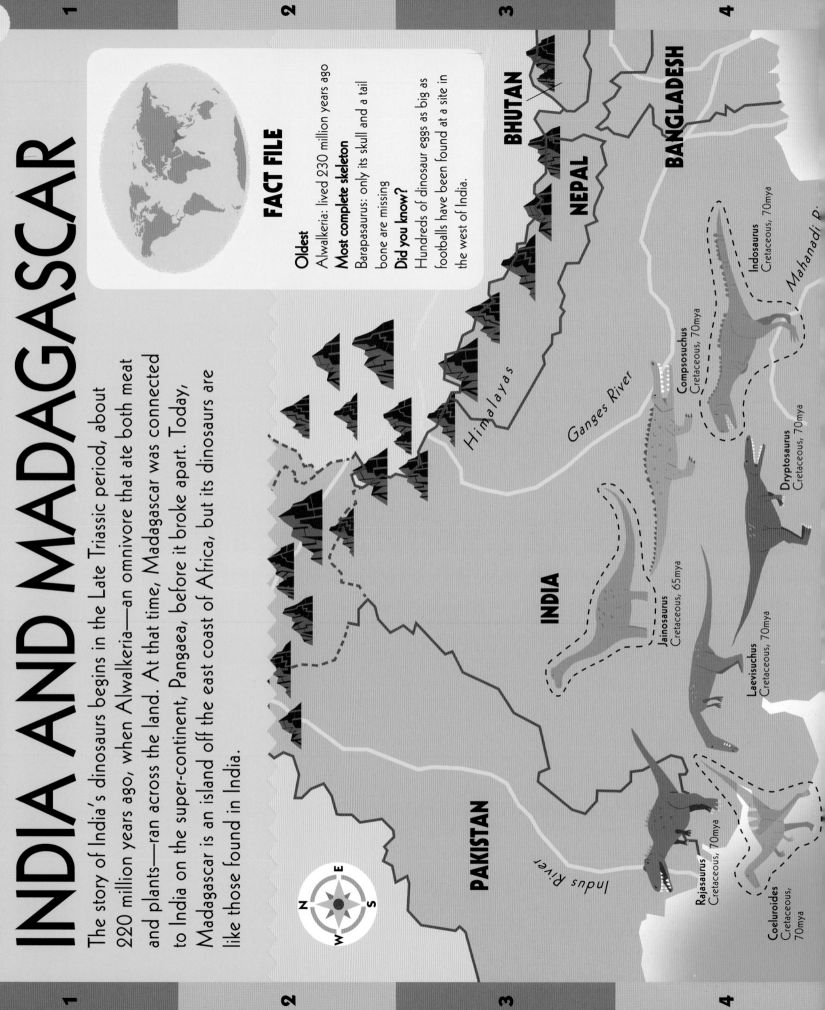

PAKISTAN

NEPAL

BHUTAN

BANGLADESH

INDIA

Himalayas

Ganges River

Indus River

Mahanadi R.

Compsosuchus
Cretaceous, 70mya

Indosaurus
Cretaceous, 70mya

Dryptosaurus
Cretaceous, 70mya

Jainosaurus
Cretaceous, 65mya

Laevisuchus
Cretaceous, 70mya

Rajasaurus
Cretaceous, 70mya

Coeluroides
Cretaceous, 70mya

N E S W

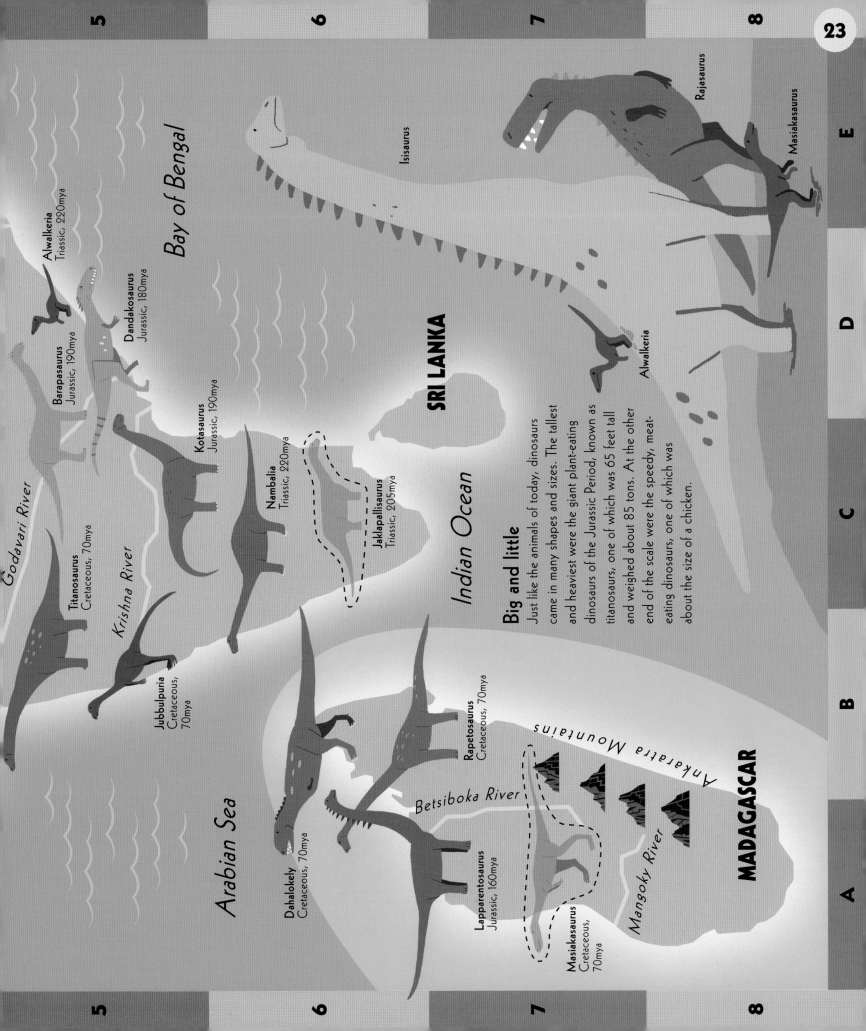

Bay of Bengal

Godavari River

Alwalkeria
Triassic, 220mya

Barapasaurus
Jurassic, 190mya

Dandakosaurus
Jurassic, 180mya

Kotasaurus
Jurassic, 190mya

Titanosaurus
Cretaceous, 70mya

Krishna River

Nambalia
Triassic, 220mya

Jaklapallisaurus
Triassic, 205mya

Jubbulpuria
Cretaceous, 70mya

SRI LANKA

Indian Ocean

Isisaurus

Rajasaurus

Masiakasaurus

Alwalkeria

Big and little

Just like the animals of today, dinosaurs came in many shapes and sizes. The tallest and heaviest were the giant plant-eating dinosaurs of the Jurassic Period, known as titanosaurs, one of which was 65 feet tall and weighed about 85 tons. At the other end of the scale were the speedy, meat-eating dinosaurs, one of which was about the size of a chicken.

Arabian Sea

Dahalokely
Cretaceous, 70mya

Rapetosaurus
Cretaceous, 70mya

Betsiboka River

Ankaratra Mountains

Lapparentosaurus
Jurassic, 160mya

Masiakasaurus
Cretaceous, 70mya

Mangoky River

MADAGASCAR

"Dinobirds"—the feathered dinosaurs

A new type of dinosaur was found in China in the 1990s—one with colorful feathers on its body and arms, like a bird. Known as "dinobirds," they were small, meat-eating dinosaurs, which could climb trees, and probably hop from branch to branch, flapping their feathery arms as they moved around. These feathered dinosaurs are the ancestors of today's birds.

Sinornithosaurus

Young Jeholosaurus

MONGOLIA

Psittacosaurus
Cretaceous, 130mya

Velociraptor
Cretaceous, 70mya

Therizinosaurus
Cretaceous, 70mya

Protoceratops
Cretaceous, 70mya

Caudipteryx
Cretaceous, 130mya

Altai Mountains

Gobi Desert

Tian Shan Mountains

CHINA

Gigantoraptor
Cretaceous, 85mya

Dilong
Cretaceous, 125mya

Plateau of Tibet

Yellow River

Shunosaurus
Jurassic, 170mya

Micropachycephalosaurus
Jurassic, 70mya

Huayangosaurus
Jurassic, 165mya

Shantungosaurus
Cretaceous, 70mya

Himalayas

Gasosaurus
Jurassic, 165mya

Mamenchisaurus
Jurassic, 150mya

Yarlung Tsango

Yangtze

Lukousaurus
Jurassic, 190mya

FACT FILE

Long neck
Mamenchisaurus: had a 49-foot neck

Longest name
Micropachycephalosaurus: meaning "small, thick-headed lizard"

Did you know?
Gasosaurus constructus was found by a company building a gas facility. Its name means "Gas Construction Lizard."

Lufengosaurus
Jurassic, 190mya

Mekong

Fossilized dinosaur poop

Confuciusornis
Cretaceous, 120mya

NORTH KOREA

SOUTH KOREA

JAPAN

Pacific Ocean

Fossil eggs

CHINA AND MONGOLIA

Some of the most spectacular dinosaur discoveries have been made in China and the Gobi Desert of Mongolia. It's not only well-preserved skeletons that are found there—the region is also famous for dinosaur eggs, nests, droppings, tracks, and footprints. Most of all, China is well-known for fossils of birdlike dinosaurs with feathers.

Sinornithosaurus fossil

From bone to stone
Most dinosaur fossils are the remains of the hardest parts of their bodies—their bones, teeth, and claws. When a dinosaur died, its body was covered by sediment. As the body rotted away, a hole was left in the sediment, which filled with minerals and then turned to stone, to make a cast fossil. This is an exact copy of the dinosaur's body parts.

AUSTRALIA

FACT FILE

First of its kind
Minmi: the first armored dinosaur

Most complete carnivore
Australovenator: Australia's best-preserved meat-eating dinosaur

NORTHERN TERRITORIES

QUEENSLAND

Austrosaurus
Cretaceous, 105mya

Muttaburrasaurus
Cretaceous,
105mya

Wintonotitan
Cretaceous,
100mya

MacDonnell Ranges

Great Divide

Minmi
Cretaceous,
119mya

WESTERN AUSTRALIA

SOUTH AUSTRALIA

Australovenator
Cretaceous, 95mya

Rhoetosaurus
Jurassic, 170mya

Rapator
Cretaceous,
105mya

Ozraptor
Jurassic, 170mya

Kakuru
Cretaceous, 125mya

Darling

NEW SOUTH WALES

Murray

Leaellynasaura
Cretaceous,
110mya

Atlascopcosaurus
Cretaceous, 115mya

VICTORIA

Serendipaceratops
Cretaceous, 120mya

Rapator

TASMANIA

AUSTRALIA

When dinosaurs were alive, Australia was joined to Antarctica, and was much closer to the South Pole than it is today. The dinosaurs that lived there were adapted to living in a cool, dark environment. For example, Leaellynasaura, a two-legged plant-eating dinosaur from the south of Australia, had big eyes that allowed it to see in dull light. Eventually, Australia broke away from Antarctica and moved north to its present position.

Minmi

Body armor

Minmi was a wide-bodied plant-eater that moved around on all fours. Its skin was covered in bony plates and spikes, which acted like body armor to protect it from the bites, claws, and kicks of a predator.

ANTARCTICA

Today, Antarctica is a frozen, ice-covered continent. But when dinosaurs roamed the Earth, the planet's climate was warmer, and Antarctica lay farther north than it does today. It was an ice-free place where dinosaurs lived in a woodland habitat. Eventually, Earth's temperature cooled, Antarctica moved south, and glaciers spread across it. Dinosaur fossils are found among scree and gravel, where ice has not covered them up.

Big and little

Australia and Antarctica began to move apart toward the end of the Cretaceous Period, about 85 million years ago. It took millions of years for the two continents to completely separate and move to where they are today. They are still moving apart, at about 3 inches a year.

Antarctopelta
Cretaceous, 70mya

Trinisaura
Cretaceous, 70mya

Morrosaurus
Cretaceous, 70mya

Dronning Maud Land

Coats Land

Ronne Ice Shelf

Palmer land

EAST ANTARCTICA

Ellsworth Land

South Pole

WEST ANTARCTICA

Marie Byrd Land

Transantarctic Mountains

Ross Ice Shelf

Mount Kirkpatrick

Cryolophosaurus
Jurassic, 190mya

Aralosaurus
Cretaceous, 85mya

Wilkes Land

Glacialisaurus
Jurassic, 185mya

Terre Adelie

George V Land

Oates Land

FACT FILE

First dinosaur
Antarctopelta: an armored dinosaur, found in 1986 on James Ross Island

Nickname
Cryolophosaurus: nicknamed "Elvisaurus," after its strange head-crest

Cryolophosaurus

Head crest
A skeleton of Cryolophosaurus ("Frozen-crested lizard") was found high up on Mount Kirkpatrick. A two-legged meat-eater, it had a crest of bone on top of its head, which may have been for display purposes.

A   B   C   D

DEATH OF THE DINOSAURS

Dinosaurs were a very successful group of animals. They lived on Earth for about 175 million years, but about 65 million years ago they died out. The big question is, what caused the extinction of the dinosaurs? Scientists have come up with several theories to explain what might have happened to them.

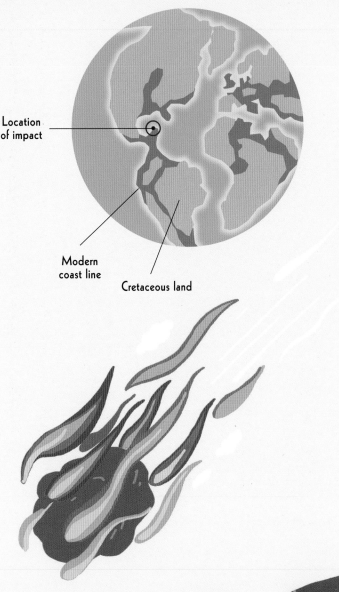

Location of impact

Modern coast line

Cretaceous land

Theory 1: Asteroid impact

In 1990 a gigantic impact crater was found at Chicxulub, on the coast of Yucatan, Mexico. It measures 112 miles across, and was made when an asteroid—a space rock —smashed into Earth about 65 million years ago. The impact would have blasted debris into the atmosphere, plunging the world into a period of darkness and acid rain. Plants would have died, so plant-eating dinosaurs and other animals would have died too. With their main source of prey gone, the meat-eating dinosaurs would have struggled to survive and slowly died out.

Impact crater

DID YOU KNOW?

The crater at Chicxulub was made by an asteroid that slammed into Earth at a speed of about 62,000 miles per hour. The space rock, which was about 6 miles across, was instantly vaporized by the force of the impact.

Quetzalcoatlus

Hypacrosaurus

A   B   C   D

Theory 2: Climate change

The dinosaurs died out because the Earth's climate changed. Scientists know that about 65 million years ago there was an increase in volcanic activity, which would have pumped carbon dioxide gas into the atmosphere. The gas might have formed a layer around the planet which stopped heat from escaping. By trapping heat, the atmosphere would have warmed up. Plants would have died, deserts would have spread, and this could have led to the death of the dinosaurs.

Theory 3: Volcanic eruptions

The extinction of the dinosaurs comes at the same time as a long period of massive volcanic eruptions in central India. Dust, ash, and gases would have been ejected high up into the atmosphere, enough to circle the globe. Sunlight would have been blotted out and this would have led to a long, cold period. Dinosaurs would have found it difficult to survive in a cold climate, so they died out.

Thick layer of ash

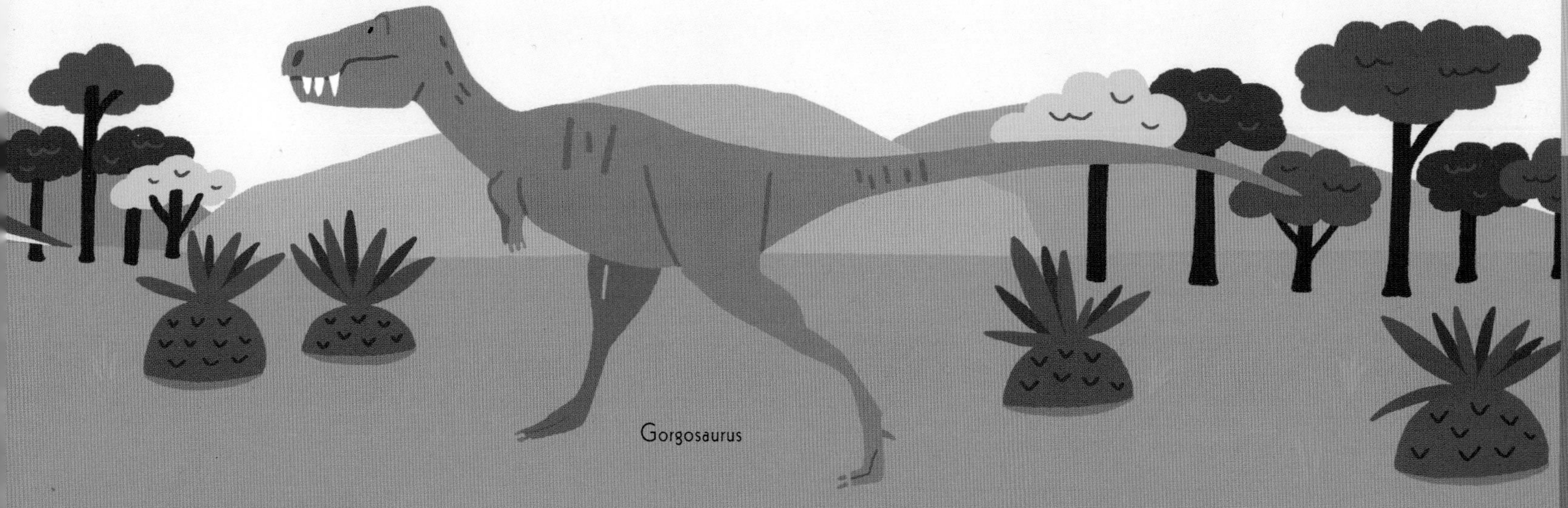

Gorgosaurus

INDEX